Podcasting for Beginners:

Start, Grow and Monetize Your Podcast

By Salvador Briggman

Copyright © 2017 Salvador Briggman LLC

All rights reserved. No part of this publication may be reproduced, distributed, or transmitted in any form or by any means, including photocopying, recording, or other electronic or mechanical methods, without the prior written permission of the publisher, except in the case of brief quotations embodied in critical reviews and certain other noncommercial uses permitted by copyright law.

Although the author and publisher have made every effort to ensure that the information in this book was correct at press time, the author and publisher do not assume and hereby disclaim any liability to any party for any loss, damage, or disruption caused by errors or omissions, whether such errors or omissions result from negligence, accident, or any other cause.

The book is not intended for use as a source of legal or financial advice. You should always consult legal and financial professionals to provide specific guidance in evaluating and pursing investment or business opportunities. The advice, examples, and strategies in this book are not suitable for every situation. The materials are not intended to represent or guarantee desired results.

http://www.podcastinghacks.com

Introduction

When I started my podcast, I was 24 years old, completely clueless about audio editing, and a ***painfully introverted*** public speaker. I was very, very meek.

To this day, I don't know why I ever thought I could actually figure out this whole podcasting thing. I ordered a cheap microphone off of Amazon, signed up for an inexpensive hosting provider, and started producing podcast episodes out of my apartment in Greenpoint, Brooklyn.

I had no idea what I was doing, and it showed. They were horrible! I must have bored my early listeners to tears!

My voice sounded like a robot. Sometimes, I would "shout" and talk like an infomercial salesman because I wanted to sound more confident. It was really bad...

There were many starts and stops. I'd be very consistent one month, and the next month I'd get lazy. Sometimes, I wondered if I was just simply wasting my time on podcasting. Maybe I wasn't meant to be a public speaker?

But, I kept at it.

I kept trying. I kept growing. Most importantly, I kept learning.

Oh boy, am I glad I did. Over the next few years, I'd go on to amass more than 150,000 downloads, develop a fan base of loyal subscribers who "binge listen" to my show, and get to interview amazing entrepreneurs, authors, and award-winning podcasters. It's been epic!

I've come to realize that it wasn't really my fault that I wasn't seeing success early on. I had the will and determination. I was even willing to invest money!

The problem was that I didn't have the training. I didn't know what to do. I didn't know how to get started. I didn't know how to get downloads, get people to listen to my show, or make money.

The one thing that I wish I had when I got started was a guide. I wanted someone who could show me the ropes, without having to invest thousands and thousands of dollars in a personal coach.

I created this guide for you, because it's the book that I wish I had available to me. The techniques, strategies, and resources that you'll discover in this guide will literally supercharge your podcast.

If you follow my advice, you'll become another breakout success and go on to develop a base of raving fans, just like I have. You just have to have that same hunger I did. You have to be willing to make this podcast a priority in your life.

- Salvador Briggman

P.S. I have a FREE video on "Podcasting Tips For Beginners."

(http://www.salvadorbriggman.com/podcastinghacksbonus)

Table of Contents

Chapter 1: Why You MUST Start a Podcast 1
Chapter 2: Crafting the Idea for Your Show 19
Chapter 3: Podcasting Equipment 28
Chapter 4: How to Launch Your Podcast 33
Chapter 5: Monetizing Your Podcast... 47
Chapter 6: Conclusion... 54

Chapter 1: Why You MUST Start a Podcast

There was a time when podcasting was relegated to the fringes of society. No one knew what a podcast was, how you listened to one, or even how to produce one.

Recently, however, podcasting has been gaining more and more steam. A recent Washington Post article reported that subscriptions to podcasts via iTunes reached 1 billion in 2013 and according to Edison Research, an estimated 39 million Americans have listened to a podcast in the past month.

What was once considered an activity restricted to only a few tech savvy people has now reached the mainstream and is gathering rapid momentum.

We've seen the rise of popular entertaining podcasts like Serial, a true-crime story, business podcasts like Entrepreneur on Fire, a show that features interviews with entrepreneurs, and even podcasts that show you how to create multiple passive streams of income online, like the Smart Passive Income podcast.

Like most people, I learned about podcasting a few years ago when the initial Apple iPod came out and hadn't thought much of it since. I considered it to be an extremely niche content medium that not many people listened to and that even fewer people produced. I never understood why someone would tune into a podcast on a topic, when they could watch a YouTube video on the subject or read an article online.

Why has podcasting become popular?

I love podcasting because, unlike YouTube, you don't need an internet connection to listen to your favorite shows. You can also download new episodes in seconds. It doesn't even take up very much space on your smartphone. I've learned so much from the podcasts that I am subscribed to and hope that I have also provided useful content on my podcast.

There are many benefits to podcasting for listeners, the podcasting community, and their sponsors. Let's look at a few of those in detail:

The Ability to Generate Revenue with Minimal Investment

Yes, podcasters do earn revenue. Some podcasts end up earning more than their creators ever could have dreamt of when they started podcasting in the first place.

Many podcasters who started small have now been able to sign lucrative five and even six figure advertising contracts. Big brands are only too eager to link their names with the leading names in the podcast industry.

To give you an idea of numbers, the Entrepreneur on Fire podcast generates $55,000 per month in sponsorship income and over $300k in total income per month. Crazy!

Let there be no doubt, this is currently a vastly untapped industry in the truest sense of the word.

It's not just the big names that are making a killing. Now even small-time players are getting contracts and sponsors. So, why do sponsors even bother with podcasts when there are many different avenues available for spending their advertising budgets?

The Convenience of Audio Content for the End Consumer

All marketers have one thing in common. They are all vying to catch someone's attention. This is the single cornerstone of marketing.

Today's net savvy generation has a tremendous amount of information available at their fingertips. With social media, texting,

Spotify, and YouTube, there are always countless distractions, all of which are competing for the attention of the end consumer.

It's hard to give your one hundred percent undivided attention to one thing at any given point in time.

This is a major reason why television advertisements are no longer that effective at selling products. If you are in the middle of a show and it takes an ad break, the odds are that you would quickly flip channels until you came across something more exciting than that ad. This means a loss to the advertiser who has spent a lot of money to place that ad in a popular prime time program. You just killed all the advertiser's efforts and hard work in a second!

The same holds true for print media and even the internet, since you can simply gloss over newspaper ads and website banners to read the content that matters to you the most.

Focusing on one thing at a time with many different distractions is virtually impossible. It's very hard to watch an ad on TV when there might be something far more exciting on another channel. The same goes for reading an article. Here lies the root cause as to why so many advertisers are now sponsoring podcasts.

The awesome thing about a podcast from the view of a potential sponsor is that the content generated is audio and available on just about any media player. This way, the listener can tune in while simultaneously doing something else, which makes it the perfect medium. He or she can be driving a car, jogging, spring cleaning, or even working out at the local gym. A podcast is a great way to brighten up even the most mundane and otherwise boring tasks. This ability to multitask makes it easy for podcast fans to listen in whenever they are doing something that does not require their complete concentration.

In fact, tuning into a podcast does not create a distraction but more of a "diversion" from their present activity. As a result, the inherent convenience and portability of audio content makes these activities more of an enriching experience.

It Builds a Loyal Audience of Fans

Podcasts essentially operate on the same principles as blogs, i.e. the core purpose is to create an ever-growing audience. While it's not possible to retain each listener tuning in for the first time, over time, many people in your target audience will tune in often enough to be classed as loyal listeners. These people will not just tune in regularly but also recommend you to their friends and peers.

It's an amazing way to build a fan base of thriving loyal subscribers who are interested in the same topic and who know, like, and trust you.

Podcasting Industry Statistics

While podcasting has been around for well over two decades, only now has it finally managed to make its presence known in many different industries. In fact, it is precisely due to this increasing popularity that brands have started sponsoring podcasts more than ever before.

This is because podcasts have been steadily gaining momentum in the past few years. Let's study some industry statistics to gain insight into up-and-coming trends and the future of podcasting as a whole:

2013 to 2016

From 2015 to 2016, podcasts grew in popularity by 23 percent (Convince and Convert). At the time, it was estimated that as many as 21 percent of all Americans twelve years of age and up had listened to at least one podcast in the previous month. This was well above the corresponding 17 percent from the same month of the previous year.

That makes it a four percent increase in the popularity of podcasting in just one year alone. However, when these same figures are compared to numbers from 2013, the figures rise far higher, up to 75 percent or so. This means that podcast listeners almost doubled within only a thirty-six-month time frame.

A staggering 3.3 billion people downloaded podcasts in 2015, an almost 200 percent increase from the 1.3 billion downloads in 2012 (Pew Research Center). There was also a corresponding 75 percent growth amongst content providers.

Now let us look at these figures in a contextual light. To understand the 21-percentage point mark we can look at the percentage of people who use Twitter, which also comes to 21 percent. In other words, as of 2016 roughly the same number of people in America listen to podcasts and use Twitter.

In terms of national population statistics, it brings the total podcast audience up to approximately 57 million people in the United States of America alone.

Why Do These Podcasting Statistics Look So Good?

One main reason behind the inherent popularity of the podcast platform is the many ways podcasts can be listened to. In the early days of the podcast revolution, many listeners were confined to their personal computers, with laptops and notebooks providing only limited mobility.

However, all podcast program consumption increased with the invention of every newer technology that allowed for a degree of mobility that had never been seen before. As a matter of fact, the recent growth spurt is driven largely by the relative ease with which many new mobile and hand-held devices have become available.

While once it was an outlier for someone to own a smartphone, now it's the contrary – if you don't own a smart phone, most people are asking you why, because it's so cheap! Smartphones make it ridiculously easy to download new podcast episodes over Wi-Fi, which you can listen to later. No more cables are needed to sync a podcast to your iPhone.

When we consider the advent of smart phones and tablets, we realize that most podcasts (64 percent) have gone through a paradigm shift with reference to their overall consumption. Now they are being listened to on these highly portable and convenient hand-held devices. This spurt in the popularity of mobile electronic media has been directly responsible for the corresponding popularity of podcasts in general.

This is because many listeners who opt to tune in to their favorite show do so only because they are able to keep their attention on not just the show itself, but also many different activities that they could do while listening to the podcast at the same time in an otherwise computer free environment.

The above figures showcase the fact that significantly increasing numbers of individuals as well as media outlets have begun to enter this space in the hopes of becoming early influencers and market leaders in this newly discovered medium. Indeed, many digital news publishers have already stated that they are or will be capitalizing on this trend.

The Expected Growth of Podcasting

The above figures alone should be convincing enough to assure you that the well over a decade long growth of podcasting is not a mere fluke, but rather a trend that is going to continue well into the foreseeable future.

The past few years are testimony to the fact that this medium has slowly but steadily been gaining a very high level of traction, at least as far as American audiences are concerned. This traction has not been lost on the creators of these podcasts or the many brands that are now clamoring to associate themselves with the more popular podcasters in cyberspace.

This popularity has now trickled down to not just the big names in the world of podcasts but also many small-time operators, who have been able to create their own audiences from scratch though their sheer diligence and personal creativity.

In fact, approximately 57 million Americans regularly tune in to their favorite podcasts and these numbers have been rising at a consistent rate from the days when podcasts were newly invented. That's a steady rise of around 23 percent per year.

Therefore, projections about the future of podcasting have been very positive especially since this is still a growing field and nowhere near saturation point. Many new people are still discovering podcasts for the first time and subsequently getting hooked in the bargain.

Where Is The Industry Going?

I think we're going to see a lot of growth in the coming years in the podcasting industry, particularly in the categories that were traditionally popular for audio tapes, CDs, and radio, like motivational speaking, learning languages, drama/stories, comedy, business advice, and more.

In addition, we're already seeing that a lot of celebrities are using podcasting to connect with their fans, from Snookie to Dave Ramsey. Eventually, once all cars are Bluetooth enabled, podcasting will be a formidable competitor to traditional broadcasting mediums like radio.

Podcasts and the Field of Sports

Back when podcasting was in its infancy and even in later years when sports podcasting was comparatively more mature, the stereotype of the sports podcast pretty much remained the same. A typical podcast chiefly consisted of a group of experts chatting while they reviewed a roundup of the week's events relating to the specific sport being covered.

Most of the time this was aimless banter that was hardly any different than many radio broadcasts. This led to considerable boredom amongst the listeners who merely tuned in to listen to the happenings from the legends of the game. Here the content was not generating listenership. Rather, it was the big names of the program hosts who still had the star power and the glamour to rope in audiences.

However, such formats could only continue for so long as even the most glamorous of sports superstars tend to lose their shine when they essentially talk about the same thing, with the same people all the time.

Enter ESPN and Its Game-Changing Strategy

Enter the sports channel ESPN and its single-handed reinvention of the sports podcast.

They have brought imaginative podcasting to the sports world and have pretty much created their very own version of the serialized format, clothed in sports garb.

ESPN has included highly addictive and thrilling stories to weave a tale-based narrative and include both new interviews as well as archival audio of some of the most thrilling moments in the world of sports. These are packaged in the form of well-established and famous audio documentaries, led by some of the leading luminaries of the podcast industry.

As the show inevitably gains popularity not just sporting bodies but an increasing number of sponsors will be forced to look at the power of podcasting in a whole new light. It is not just ESPN that will benefit but podcasting itself will get a much-needed boost. The show's popularity is ushering in users who have never even heard a podcast before but (thanks to the thrilling audio documentaries of their favorite sports and stars) are now tuning in for show after show.

The result is a new strategy for monetizing the archives of content that is owned by a specific brand (in this case ESPN).

This in turn easily generates more content as it forces both sporting bodies and brands to take a whole new look at the tremendous power of podcasting. Undoubtedly, this is leading to many a boardroom brain storming session regarding their whole content strategy approach.

For the industry, it will end up having the following benefits:

- It will help generate the groundwork for building assets that would be highly desirable for sponsors who are always on the lookout for both fresh and original content

- Thanks to this strategy, sports would not be restricted only to specific seasons and the audience and sponsors now would have access to marketable content all year-long

- Such podcasts will ultimately lure away many sports fans from mainstream and traditional broadcasters to the podcast itself and thereby confirm podcasts as a highly disruptive technology

- Ultimately, such trail blazing podcasts would provide a high quality as well as very cost-effective method to leverage old audio that may have been languishing in the archives for lack of listeners. Meanwhile, different talents may come to the fore when such audio clips are dusted off and presented by new media savvy podcasters

- Finally, such a podcast would easily deliver a great marketing product that not only can go 'viral' but would have a longer shelf life than its counterparts in the broadcasting world.

The Untapped Potential of Ever More Listeners

The key reason why podcasts are so popular is the fact that many podcasters can weave a spell around their respective audiences. In plain and simple language, a typical listener ends up getting hooked to the podcasts he listens to on a regular basis. This holds true not just for American listeners, but also their counterparts all over the developed world.

If we study podcast viewer details from different countries, we realize that listeners who live in the United Kingdom tend to listen to over 6 hours per week (Rajar). These statistics are close to those in Australia, where people like to tune in for an average of 5.5 hours per week (ABC).

We have already discussed podcast listening statistics in the USA which show that an estimated 20 percent of the current population is tuning in on a regular basis. That may be a lot of people, but it also means that 80 percent of the population does not listen to podcasts at all.

This is a veritable gold mine of an untapped market with near limitless potential for virtually endless growth. The opportunity for conversion is simply too immense to be ignored. These remaining people can be brought into the 'podcast fold' so to speak, it just takes some effort and dedication to grab their interest.

As a matter of fact, most radio listeners are not even aware of the fact that there exists a Netflix version of the radio that is able to both create and deliver content on demand. But as time passes, more people will realize this and ditch the mainstream medium for the world of demand generated and driven podcasts. This will be in the form of a 'life changing' discovery for them. Once they have made this change, there will be no going back to the era of traditional radio again.

TV Networks and the Era of the Podcast

In the coming years, most TV networks themselves will play a key role in ensuring that their viewers also watch their companion podcasts. It is not that they have much of a choice. Like the Polaroid and Kodak camera people who did not change with the times, if they do not do so, TV networks will simply fade into obscurity once their viewers start following podcasts.

This is because their competitors in the media will simply take the initiative to drive them out of business by appropriating their sponsors and by extension, advertising revenues when their viewers start following their competitors' podcasts. This will be possible not just though the creation of multiple companion podcasts but also through exclusive interviews as well as access to insider commentaries of popular serials and their expected story lines.

The Game of Thrones is a prime example of this trend as many podcasters have taken to discussing at length, the various twists and turns that are expected from current and upcoming episodes of the series.

In this way, podcasts will make sure that fans of highly popular shows will not have to wait until the next week to get their 'fix' regarding any information based on that show. This is not restricted only to period serials and dramas, but even popular documentaries, reality shows, and even current affairs programs.

Increasingly Seamless Connectivity

The increasing proliferation of vehicles being equipped with entertainment systems that include both Apple's Car Play as well as Android Auto is another major driver of growth of the podcast industry.

No doubt, books and informational products on tape were a huge hit several generations ago. While commuters were traveling to work they could become an expert in a new topic or pick up a foreign language. Bluetooth-enabled cars allow drivers to easily sync and listen to podcasts that they have stored on their smartphone and is replacing the earlier method of purchasing informational CDs or tapes.

More than 200 models of different vehicles are already due to roll out in the coming years. Every one of them will be equipped with media players and operating systems that take in-car entertainment to a whole new level. No more listening to boring CD music when you can easily listen to a podcast from your favorite host. This will make even the longest of drives a truly remarkable experience.

Unlike an FM radio station, there is no need to worry regarding signals and coverage area when you are going for a long drive as is a common complaint with FM radio stations. With an entertainment system fully capable of managing and downloading podcasts, you will be able listen to your favorite show regardless of whichever state you may be driving in.

As a matter of fact, even Amazon has jumped into the fray by making their 'Alexa' platform ideal for many vehicle-based infotainment systems. This is all exceptionally good news to the podcast industry. Its outreach is increasing at an extremely high pace and this has prompted many different sponsors to consider podcasting as an option when before they were only concerned with the mainstream media.

Podcasting Success Stories

Podcasting really hit the major leagues when Mar Maron finally landed an interview with the then, US President Barak Obama back in the Summer of 2015 for his "WTF" podcast.

Ever since that episode ran in June, "WTF," went on to make history by effectively becoming one of the most well-known podcasts currently available on the internet. In fact, directly after that landmark interview, an average of between 200,000 to 300,000 additional downloads were recorded per episode, as per producer Brendan McDonald, who co-created the podcast along with Maron.

"I don't believe podcasting will replace traditional radio, but I believe it will serve as another option for people who are becoming increasingly used to a wide variety of media choices," - Brendon McDonald in an email to CBS MoneyWatch

He (Brandon McDonald) was pragmatic enough to explain that Netflix may not replace all broadcast TV, but nevertheless it will be a sort of counterbalance to the near overwhelming popularity of mainstream electronic media as it exists today. The same goes for podcasting.

It is not just Maron alone. Many other highly popular influencers such as Jesse Thorn and Adam Carolla have jumped on the podcast bandwagon and have gone on to show that podcasting can be highly lucrative. Their experiences show how podcasting can be a vehicle to runaway popularity (through live shows for instance) that can be leveraged into other rewarding avenues.

Jesse Thorn's MaximumFun.org is another example of a profitable podcasting endeavor. It started off with humble beginnings after the man sold a 1963 Dodge Dart to be able to purchase a 'run of the mill' sound mixer and a pair of microphones. His informational shows started gaining popularity due to his crisp and to-the-point format. In time, he gathered literally hundreds of thousands of followers for his episodic podcasts.

Adam Carolla, is yet another highly successful podcast story. Carolla is a stand-up comedian who was very popular due to his tongue-in-cheek humor and a tendency to lampoon politicians and other famous people on both TV and radio.

He ditched the mainstream media to create his own studio in which he pumped an estimated $175,000 dollars. Initially, he did have to struggle with it, as his fans on mainstream media were not interested in making the jump to listening to podcasts. It was directly due to this reason that for first year and a half he was in the red. However, with time his profits showed a steady increase until he was generating literally millions of dollars in revenue thanks to his hit "Adam Carolla Show."

"Audio is a superior medium to terrestrial radio in that it is free to the listener, has no FCC content restrictions, no annoying 10-

minute ad blocks and is available on demand wherever and whenever on each and every digital device you may have ... This form of broadband content featuring artists programming themselves for the enjoyment of their audience is only going to continue to grow in my opinion as more and more prominent artists come into the medium." - John Carolla

Many top-ranking podcasts have pretty much turned the fortunes of their host(s) regarding their paying careers. In fact, some of the more popular podcasts can easily earn up to and over $50,000 dollars per episode.

A popular podcast known as "This American Life" garners around eight hundred thousand to one million downloads per episode on average. Now when we account for the advertising rates of the podcast medium, we find out that in the USA alone they average out at approximately $25-50 dollars per 1000 listeners. Therefore, this podcast would easily be able rake in a bare minimum of $50,000 or so per episode.

The revenue generating model for different types of podcasts varies from show to show due to many different factors. These may include the popularity of the host, a well-known guest (as we saw in the president Obama episode) or the kind of entertainment or information that the podcast provides on a standalone basis (i.e. Not being backed by advertising campaigns in the mainstream media). However, as a rule, they typically fall into either one or more of the following categories:

- Cross selling different products and services
- Listener donations
- Advertising

Cross Selling

The cross selling of many different goods and services has always been one of the mainstays of podcast revenue earning methods.

Many companies and brands see podcasts as a vehicle that will help drive traffic to their own products. We have before us the example of a brand known as the "Planet money T-shirt." They came up with a highly innovative and truly unique Planet Money T-Shirt project.

Basically, they sold $625,000 dollars' worth of T-shirts via an interesting series of podcast episodes with reference to the making of the T-shirts. From growing the cotton, processing the yarn, and container transport all the way to the delighted end users. Every process was methodically explained in individual episodes of the podcast. The series garnered a lot of support and the listeners lapped up the T-shirts as soon as they were manufactured.

Listener Donations

This concept is self-explanatory in nature. Many podcasters who are convinced of the solidness of the content they produce, confidently solicit donations from their listeners.

While this may not be the main revenue puller for many podcasts, it does nevertheless allow them to get by on an episode to episode basis until they move on into the mainstream podcast market.

You can use a website like Patreon to accomplish this!

Advertising

Podcasts start attracting advertising from sponsors once the podcast's popularity reaches a certain threshold.

Basically, the advertiser is willing to pay a predetermined fee that is loosely centered around how many listeners the podcast has in a typical episode.

Such advertisers usually use a 'promo code' so as to be able to determine precisely how successful an advertising campaign has been regarding the conversion rate of the promotion. Conversion rates basically mean the 'conversion' of the casual listener from simply listening in to becoming an actual buyer of the product.

Monetary Success

The final two podcasting success stories I want to cover are those of John Lee Dumas of EOFire and Pat Flynn of Smart Passive Income.

John Lee Dumas, creator of Entrepreneur on Fire, interviews entrepreneurs 7-days a week and has grown a podcast that generates over 1 million monthly listens. He wasn't always a successful entrepreneur and podcaster though. Before discovering the podcasting industry, Dumas took several twists and turns in his career, including spending time in the US Army, Law School, and working for a New York City start-up.

In 2016, 34% of the revenue John Lee Dumas generated came from podcasting. This adds up to $898,631! Considering that John has a 7-day a week podcast, he has a lot of advertising inventory, but it's still very impressive.

Pat Flynn of Smart Passive Income is another person whose luck was changed forever by podcasting. After being laid off from his job in architecture in 2008, Flynn started learning how to earn passive income to support his family. Now, he shares his experience and strategies in a weekly podcast that has garnered over 33 million total downloads on his website.

In December of 2016, Pat earned $6,931 from podcast sponsors for his two shows, the Smart Passive Income podcast, and the Ask Pat podcast. Extrapolated out, this would be more than $80,000 per year. He's publicly stated that advertising or making the most money that he can from the show is not his primary objective. His business as a whole generated $151,137.88 in the month of December.

My Personal Podcast Statistics: 2015 to 2016 to 2017

November 2015 is the first month where my podcast cracked the 3,000 download count.

I released 9 new episodes in November 2015, which represented 65% of the podcast's total downloads for the month.

Between October and November, the total podcast downloads grew by 28%.

Here are the factors that I think are responsible for the massive growth during this time period:

- Frequency: after doubling the frequency of my podcast, I saw much more growth.
- Titling: I got better at titling episodes in terms of what the listener will get out of listening to each podcast episode.
- Teasing: I did YouTube videos and periscopes to "tease" episodes and convince viewers to check out specific podcast episodes.

I have no doubts that titling and teasing have a huge impact on podcast downloads. I think it's very similar to the YouTube marketplace. If you title a video well or have a great thumbnail, it prompts clicks. Same goes for blog posts and podcasts.

Basically, the name of the game for my podcast (though your category or subject may differ), is lots of new useful content.

In 2015, my podcast had 20,880 total downloads.

There was a spike in the second half of the year when I decided to take podcasting more seriously. I set up a regular schedule and really started to work to produce quality content.

I worked to improve my speaking voice. I was more conscious of the guests that I brought on. I really tried to deliver as much value as possible on every podcast episode.

In 2016, my podcast had 58,285 downloads.

That's an increase of 179%!

Pretty cool, huh?

In 2017, my podcast has already surpassed the 2016 numbers and it's anticipated I will close out the year with more than 80,000 downloads.

That's an increase of 37%!

Now, which devices are my downloads coming from?

According to Libsyn, the majority of my downloads are coming from AppleCoreMedia, iTunes, itunesstored, and PodcastAddict. Chrome, Safari, Mozilla, and Firefox are also big contributors.

According to my calculations, about 19% of my downloads are coming from a web browser. That's pretty surprising, right?!

These statistics are a testament to the fact that podcasting is alive and well. People are actually listening to my voice! In fact, more than 150,000 people around the world have heard my voice. I even now have people on my show who have "binge listened" to my podcast.

The Crowdfunding Demystified podcast is now one of the main ways that new followers discover my work online. It's the direct result of thousands of dollars in revenue and massive product launches. I've improved so much as speaker since starting my show. I've also gotten really good at marketing, sales, and interviewing. It's funny to think that I'm just a young dude in his apartment talking into a microphone. Weird, right?

Whether you're just vaguely interested in podcasting, or you want to create the next hit show, it's not too late to submit your podcast to iTunes and join this new wave!

Chapter 2: Crafting the Idea for Your Show

When starting a podcast, you need to decide what type of show you want to create. Podcasts can be either informational, entertaining, or both.

Here you'll have to determine precisely what target market you want to focus on and how. For this, it's important to understand the key differences between the two types of shows mentioned above.

If you choose to start an informational podcast, you need a storehouse of information and expertise available to get through not just a single episode but an entire season's worth. 'One off' podcasts rarely (if ever) generate revenues.

On the other hand, creating an entertaining podcast also requires planning ahead. You need to have certain story boards in mind. Story boards can be based on a variety of themes, from family oriented dramas to arguably one of the most difficult genres to master, i.e. comedy.

Entertaining Podcasts

Entertainment (especially comedy) requires a certain aptitude and talent to make it worthwhile for listeners to tune in on a weekly basis, episode after episode and season after season. If you have that "knack" go for it. Let us study the following examples:

My Brother, My Brother, and Me!

My Brother, My Brother, and Me! is an 'advice show' for the media savvy listener of the 21st century. The podcast is hosted by three actual brothers who use the term 'advice' with their tongues held firmly in their cheeks (so to speak).

As a matter of fact, just about every episode of the podcast commences with a well-intentioned warning to the effect that their "advice should never be followed." This is in large part because this 'band of brothers' (Justin, Griffin and Travis McElroy) are by no means counselors or professional psychologists. In fact, they're not even consultants to begin with.

They are quite simply just three brothers who love to have a good hearty laugh and that's precisely what makes this show so engaging and popular. The three brothers go through each episode by answering a mixed bag of questions selected from the many different queries they get from audience members. Sometimes they interpose popular questions from Yahoo Answers to add a bit of variety to the show.

However, the format is such that they end up diverting from the topic and just plain kidding around with each other in a manner unique to brothers. The unmistakable camaraderie they share with each other can easily be identified as both genuine and easy going. The vibe of the show makes the listener feel equally comfortable with the brothers as they are with each other. This is one of the most endearing qualities that has led to the success of this highly entertaining podcast.

If you can create such comedic gold in the podcast world, then do so. However, the gaiety must come naturally. You should not try to force it. The audience members will pick it up and will not be interested in your show regardless of how hard you try. That's why if comedy isn't your strong suit you may want to switch to an informational podcast on a subject in which you have near absolute mastery.

Informational Podcasts

Informational podcasts teach listeners about a specific topic in a way that's both factual and framed to capture the audience's interest.

Suppose you're a firearms enthusiast and have spent a lifetime living amongst other equally enthusiastic individuals who love firearms with the same passion that you do.

You can start a firearms podcast with nothing but a couple of microphones with a computer that has access to the internet.

Different Examples and Ideas for Informational Podcasts

Here, you don't need fancy equipment or long elaborate story boards. All you need is the knowledge that you already hold in your own head. For example, you can do a podcast episode on wheel guns' vs pistols and the pros and cons for conceal carrying either one or both. You can ask guests for their opinion, such as local police officers who carry a firearm in the line of duty.

Other ideas may include episodes on copper jacketed projectiles and their effects on barrel wear and tear in comparison to steel jacketed ones or a few episodes on stopping power such as the 9mm hollow point vs the venerable .45 ACP ball ammo.

You can also do an audience inspired 'Gun of the Week' review based on answers you receive from polls where you ask the audience to select the weapon they want reviewed.

Alternately, you can even hold a live fire exercise at the local shooting range to ascertain the power and accuracy of (for example) a rifled sabot slug at hundred yards or beyond. The sound of the wind and other shooters at the range would add a touch of authenticity to the whole exercise.

The possibilities and combinations are as endless as the number of gun enthusiasts that you may want to target. In time, major gun and accessories manufacturers may be interested in sponsoring your show or advertising on it as well. You can even call the marketing representatives of manufacturing companies who might want to launch a new weapon on your podcast.

Another example would be the Planet T-Shirt series of podcasts that we alluded to earlier. By sharing the different steps of the manufacturing process of their T-shirts from start to finish, not only did they provide information regarding the cotton and garments industry, they also simultaneously created demand for their products with the same podcast series.

Creating the Format (Duration, Frequency, Guests)

The format of a typical podcast is one of the most important things that you must consider before the launch of your very own show.

Too long a podcast would invariably create boredom, while too short a show would not be able to gather the impact that you may wish to garner. Here the "Goldilocks Principle" holds the show together. You must find that not too long and not too brief 'sweet spot' that would keep your audience well and thoroughly hooked.

Also of key importance is the frequency of the podcast. Here too an overly elongated time frame in between episodes would mean that the podcast would seep from the active consciousness of the listeners and they would inevitably lose interest. On the other hand, too many shows in too short a time frame would lead to overkill. The audience would simply become bored and look for information and entertainment elsewhere

The process of introducing guests to your podcast should also be organized. Before a famous personality (in media or politics, for instance) is slated to address the show, the podcaster should create hype by informing the audience as to the eminent arrival of the guest. You can state that on this and this episode Mr. or Mrs. XYZ would be invited and then start counting down the episodes before the pivotal one.

This works way better then 'springing' a well-known surprise guest at an audience that is not mentally prepared for him. Not only would all the listeners not be tuned in at that point in time, they also wouldn't be able to inform their friends and family who may not be listeners of the podcast but fans of that distinguished guest speaker.

A case in point would be that of the podcast with the American president. It did not happen out of the blue, but rather it involved a lot of background work and the audience was simply taken off its feet. This led to a huge jump in listeners both during the hype creation stage as well as immediately after the talk show.

However, a podcast does not necessarily have to feature the American president to make a difference in the listener ratings.

Provided the marketing and hype created has done its job effectively, even relatively minor celebrities can get the job done. This can be easier for entertaining podcasts, since a celebrity may be well-known to the non-podcast listening community. Having a celebrity guest on your show would be a great way to get people who don't currently listen to podcasts to tune in as well.

A movie or TV star or a standup comic may be an ideal addition to your show if it's an entertainment podcast. On the other hand, for an informational podcast, it would make more sense to go for an expert in a specific field. He or she may not generate as much interest amongst the masses as an entertainment or showbiz related celebrity, but that's okay. Your listeners would be more likely to tune in to an expert if they're seeking information on a topic, which may be why you have created an informational podcast in the first place.

The easiest way to determine an appropriate length and frequency is to listen to other shows in your category. For me, I'm used to a 30 to 60-minute podcast, as I listen to shows about business, life, and personal development. These shows will usually post once a week. I tend to be more interested in the episodes that star guests.

Acquiring and Handling Feedback from Listeners

Acquiring and handling feedback from listeners is another important step to building a successful podcast. Completing this step will help give you an idea as to how your listeners perceive your podcast. This is crucial when it comes to determining your future course of action such as the kind of guests you will invite or what content you will share with your audience in future episodes. You can solicit suggestions/advice and any other kind of feedback that you deem desirable to increase your number of listeners.

By including your target audience in the production process, you give them a clearly visible means of participation in your programming. This way, not only do you succeed in creating a sense of 'ownership' amongst the target audience but you also ensure that they remain hooked, to ascertain just how many of their suggestions have been followed. By catering to the whims and fancies of your listeners you make sure that your pool of loyalist viewers does not decrease.

Such feedback can be gathered in the following ways:

Though the Phone

This is the simplest method. All you need to do is listen in to the audience members and jot down their suggestions. Implement the best ones while discarding those that are not feasible.

Though the Mail or Email

Suggestions can be sent to your email address or even a P.O box should your audience be wide enough to include people who eschew email in favor of snail mail.

Though Social Media, iTunes, or On Your Website

This is arguably the trickiest form of feedback collection because other users can see the suggestions and advice. Audience members might want to see their own ideas to be implemented first and foremost. Moreover, listeners will want to be informed as to why precisely you have refrained from following their advice, if that is the case.

This needs to be handled in such a way that it doesn't create any dissatisfaction. You don't want listeners to leave negative comments on your page or share those same comments in groups, communities, or their own social media pages. A negative comment is likely to garner far more interest than a positive one. If a negative comment goes viral it will certainly affect the popularity of your show.

Here the 'worst' thing you can do would be to simply delete all negative posts from your home page or profile. This would not only create a fake and all too positive image but the people who have written negative comments could take screen shots and pass them on until they become viral. This would have a severely adverse effect on the overall popularity of your show.

Dealing with Discontentment

Implementing one suggestion while ignoring others can create feelings of jealously amongst your most loyal listeners. Therefore, you must be highly diplomatic when dealing with all suggestions on social media or on your website. You must acknowledge them all and apologize to people whose feedback you cannot incorporate into your show while giving clear reasons as to why. You need to appear genuinely regretful as much as possible.

As for the people whose feedback you do decide to incorporate into your future shows, the fact that their suggestions have made it on your podcast is good enough.

Highlighting listeners whose ideas you've chosen on social media, your site, or on your show can be a good way to boost engagement. Thanking them long after the show is over is not necessary, though. This would make them feel entitled to give you advice that they insist must be followed, which can curb your freedom to quite an extent when it comes to running your show the way you want to.

How to Come Up a "Good" Show Idea

The most important part of success in podcasting (or any other area of life) comes down to one thing, execution! The rewards in business and life go to those who are consistently taking action towards their goals.

I've had friends who have come up with pretty "cool" show ideas, but they don't take any action to make them a reality. They stay "ideas" forever.

Everyone can come up with a "good" show that addresses a profitable niche or one that sounds unique, quirky, or innovative. You might of it after you've had a cup of coffee with a friend. You'll pat yourself on the back for how brilliant it sounds. Then, you'll forget it about it in a week's time.

A good idea starts with the podcaster. What are your interests? What are you passionate about? What are you good at? Who are you?

You're more likely to stick with a show idea that you like and are passionate about. It won't fizzle out, because you enjoy it. Even though it takes some work to produce, it's basically effortless, because you love it!

Of course, you should do a little bit of market research. You have to assess demand for the individual topic and who's already advertising in the marketplace. But, at the same time, if you want to see a show that discusses a particular topic, chances are that there are other people out there just like you. You just need to find them.

When I started my show, I figured there would be demand because I write a blog on the same subject. I didn't know if people would be interested in long interviews, but I decided to try it because I was passionate about the subject.

I made the commitment to create 25 podcast episodes and then assess whether or not I'd continue with the show. Now, I'm on episode #184, and I'm happy I tried it out!

Chapter 3: Podcasting Equipment

Every The most intimidating part of podcasting for beginners is all of the equipment that's required to get started with podcasting. Thankfully, much of this is overhyped by audio engineers who are enthusiastic about audio quality to the point where they'll tell you that you need a ton of stuff for the perfect sounding show.

In reality, you don't need that much fancy equipment in order to get started. Some of the most popular shows out there don't even use a premium microphone. Tim Ferriss, a popular podcaster, is famous for using a simple $64 Audio-Technica microphone.

When it comes to podcasting equipment, there is a lot of terminology that can make your head spin. Do you need a condenser microphone? Do you need a mixer? What kind of software should you use?

With this chapter, I'm going to walk you through a simple podcasting setup, along with taking you behind the scenes to my own podcasting setup which has generated over 100,000 show downloads.

Before we get started, you need to put your finger on how you'll record this show.

How Will You Record Guests?

Your answer to this question will guide your equipment choices going forward. For example, if you intend to conduct interviews online via Skype, then you're going to need a microphone that is USB compatible.

However, if you intend to do most of your interviews live, then you might need to think more about the sound environment, how you'll capture two audio files, and the easiest microphone to use for your guest.

Some shows are more video-based and the actual iTunes podcast is more of an afterthought. For these types of podcasts, you might need a high-quality lapel microphone that will produce great sounding audio for the video. Then, you might do some editing to extract the audio file from the video and put it up on iTunes.

When you figure out how you'll conduct guest interviews, it will make everything easier going forward.

Top 5 Podcasting Microphones

There are many microphones that you can choose from when getting started with podcasting. I'm going to be referencing some of the most popular and affordable ones that will get you up to speed fast. These are great if you want to start an educational show like mine where you interview guests via Skype. They're also great for entertaining shows.

Audio-Technica ATR2100 USB Microphone

This microphone comes highly recommended by John Lee Dumas and Tim Ferriss, both of which are extremely popular podcasters. It's an affordable and high-quality USB microphone that produces a great sound. It also has over 600 customer reviews on Amazon, most of them positive.

While not the highest end mic on the market, it's a great entry-level starter microphone for a podcaster who wants something better than their computer or smartphone headset.

For a price of $59.00, I think it's hard to beat the value that the ATR2100 delivers.

Blue Yeti

I might get some pushback on this, but I'm going to be recommending the Blue Yeti as my second starter podcasting microphone on this list! And yes, this is what I use.

The reason I decided to purchase this mic was twofold. First, I like that it has gain and volume control on the microphone. You can easily mute the mic and it also allows you to hear how you sound with a great headphone jack. Second, it has over 3,000 reviews on Amazon, most of them positive.

The one downside of the Blue Yeti is that it's very sensitive. It can sometimes pick up the humming of your computer or any movements that you make while you're recording. Overall, this mic has a great quality and has some great audio controls for new podcasters, but it does come in at a higher price tag.

Right now, it's $124.00 on Amazon.

Blue Snowball USB Microphone

This is another frequently used mic that I see beginning podcasters and YouTubers use to augment their audio quality. I find though that almost everyone will upgrade from it at some point.

Aside from being a USB mic, one of the great things about the Blue Snowball is that it's extremely affordable, coming in at $69.00.

The Blue Snowball has 2,000 reviews, many of them positive. One negative bit of feedback is that, "I went through two of these things, and here's the deal. If you are going to be two inches from it, or you are going to be recording loud sources, you'll be pleased as punch.

If you are going to be recording the normal volume of a human voice, or you want to record a number of participants around a table, you will find that the recording levels are just far too low."

30

To be honest, this is going to be true of many microphones out there. I've done live podcasts with my microphone and it didn't have an issue picking up the sound, but if you're far away from the source, I'd recommend using a headset with each speaker or a microphone that you can pin to your clothing.

Headset Microphones

Sometimes, it's annoying to have to speak into a standing microphone. I'm going to highlight two different headsets that you can use to record your podcast.

First, you can use the Audio-Technica BPHS1. This is what Lewis Howes uses on The School of Greatness. It's on the expensive side, but the sound quality is great!

You don't have to go all expensive though. You can also grab a Logitech headset microphone like the ClearChat Comfort/USB Headset, which is only $24.99.

You might not be 100% pleased with the sound quality, but if you're just looking to see whether or not podcasting is for you and want to try out doing a few episodes, I think this could suffice.

Heil PR-40 Dynamic Studio Recording Microphone

The last microphone that I'm going to be recommending in this list is the Heil PR-40 for high end podcasters. This is NOT for beginners in my opinion.

One Amazon review reads, "The Heil PR40 is a fantastic mic. Just do your research and make sure you understand what it can and can't do. If you're looking for an all-around studio microphone for recording music, this probably isn't the mic for you. But, if you're looking for something with which to record voiceovers, chances are you won't beat the PR40 without spending a whole lot more money."

Again, this microphone is specific for voiceovers and podcasting. It does have a steep price tag at $327.00 but delivers a quality and professional audio experience!

What About The Rest of Your Setup?

If you're just getting started with podcasting, I would not recommend making your setup super complicated. Just go with a decent sounding microphone and start making episodes!

There are two reasons for this. The first is that the main reason people FAIL at podcasting is now due to the audio quality. It's because they're not consistent. They don't stick with it. Quite frankly, many don't even get started.

I don't want you to go out there and buy a bunch of equipment that you'll never use or that won't make a difference in the early stage of your show.

The second reason is that in order fully have a rich-sounding show, you also need to be good at speaking. You can have the highest quality audio in the world, but if your voice is boring, then it doesn't matter!

Once you improve your speaking and you have a feel for how podcasting works, then you can begin to invest in higher quality audio equipment. This way, you'll get the best return on your investment and you won't waste time on things that don't matter in the early stages.

Something that WILL make a massive difference in whether or not your show is successful is how you launch it. That's what I'm going to be covering next.

Chapter 4: How to Launch Your Podcast

Once you have your concept ready and you've committed to producing the first few shows, it's time to methodically build and launch the podcast itself. This is an enormous endeavor that can make your head spin. Where should you even get started?

In this chapter, I'm going to go over some strategies that you can follow to make this process easier.

How to Set Up Your Podcast in iTunes

Whether you want to start a discussion-based podcast, interview people in your industry, or share what you've learned about a specific topic, it's a must to have your podcast in iTunes! These steps will help you get your podcast into the iTunes store:

1. Create a Name, Thumbnail Image, and Website.

The name that you choose for the podcast should be available as a domain name so that you don't run into any issues when you begin to build out your website with episodes or other forms of content. Be sure to check that first!

After you've chosen your name, I recommend setting up either a WordPress website using the guide below or set up a website using Wix:

(http://www.salvadorbriggman.com/how-to-make-a-wordpress-website-step-by-step/)

Ultimately, I think you'll find that it pays big dividends to set up your own website now, rather than having to do that later.

Although you can set up a podcast using SquareSpace rather than using your own website in addition to a specific podcast hosting provider, I've gotten some negative vibes about it from

- Tennis
- Positive masculinity
- Spiritual evolution
- Being yourself (getting paid to be yourself)

other people in the industry. SquareSpace's website creation tool is fantastic, but I think there still needs to be more work done on their podcasting functionality.

Finally, it's important to create a compelling thumbnail image. You could hire a contractor on 99designs to do this or use Fiverr if you are on the cheaper side. I personally used the Pixlr graphic design tool to create my own. Don't forget that the image must be 1400 x 1400 pixels and a maximum size of 2048 x 2048 pixels.

2. Choose a Company to Host Your Podcast

Although you can technically host your own podcast on your web server, it's best to use a third-party tool for simplicity's sake. This method will minimize downtime and make sure that your episodes can be accessed on a consistent basis, no matter the bandwidth.

I use Libsyn to host my podcast, though you can also use SoundCloud, BuzzSprout, Podbean, or Blubrry. My main qualm when setting up my show was dependability. I settled on Libsyn because they've been around for a while and cultivated an image as a stable provider. However, BuzzSprout seems to have a much better ease of use and user interface and SoundCloud has more of a social community containing other podcasters and musicians.

Of course, it depends how often you will launch your podcast episodes and the length of those episodes, but I've found podcast hosting to be relatively cheap and on par with hosting a high-quality website.

3. Submit Your Podcast to iTunes

After you've chosen the company with which you'd like to host your podcast and uploaded an episode, you submit the RSS of your podcast to iTunes. First, click on the "submit podcast" button in the podcasts category of the iTunes store.

Next, you must enter the Podcast's feed URL and proceed. After you've completed the process, your podcast will appear in the iTunes store for download once it's approved!

Your Topic Affects Your Marketing

Once you have the infrastructure of your podcast set up, you'll need to come up with an effective marketing strategy.

You might not like to hear this, but a lot of products, shows, and internet personalities that seem like they're super good at marketing actually have a marketing mechanism built into their end product.

What do I mean by that?

Let's take Andrew Warner, Tim Ferriss or even Howard Stern as examples. While it's true that they do have some marketing clout on their own, they've been able to successfully leverage the influence of their guests to fuel the growth of their podcast or audio show.

When an episode goes live, they don't solely have to rely on their own marketing platform. Their guests also share it with their followers, potentially doubling the listenership.

This might seem like a trivial distinction, but the niche that you're going after and the type of content that you intend to produce as a podcast (entertaining, informational, news) will impact how it will be shared on the web and the best way to go about marketing it.

Choose Your Marketing Platform

I think that people always try to make this step overly complex. The question you need to answer is: Where does your target audience hang out?

Do they already listen to podcasts?

Are they always on Twitter, sharing updates and following interesting people?

Do they interact and share a lot on Facebook?

Are they Instagram lovers? Maybe they spend a lot of time on Snapchat?

They might spend a lot of time just googling new and interesting things?

Unfortunately, you can't expect your target listeners to come to you. You need to go to them and the platforms they use.

My marketing platform is my blog's email list, social media accounts, and blog posts.

Start Generating Hype

The next question is: how can you possibly build an audience when you're in the process of launching your very first podcast? The best way is to generate hype. Get creative. Something along the lines of "A big new wave is headed your way on Sunday December 27, 2018" could be an interesting tag line. The goal is to make people curious as to what your podcast is all about.

You can share this tagline on different online platforms like Facebook and Twitter. Just make sure that you mention something about the main topic around which you will be creating your series of podcasts. You can even go offline and use print media (such as magazines and periodicals that are read by your target audience) to further your reach.

In terms of online marketing, keep in mind that the process will be the same as it is for any other product. You must use various platforms and tools to create a sense of curiosity among your target audience. Subsequently, you can exploit their curiosity to your advantage in order to increase your fan base. All of this can easily be done on a relatively small budget.

I'll go through some simple but effective ways to generate hype for your podcast.

Social Media Scheduling and Automation

There are a slew of social media platforms and bookmarking websites out there including:

Twitter: A great platform to broadcast messages to a large audience, reach out to journalists, and network with companies or individuals in your niche.

Facebook: Facebook is a powerful tool for staying in touch with your network and your followers. I personally do not like Facebook business pages because of the ranking algorithm which determines whether your post is seen by the number of people who have "liked" your page (unless you pay). In other words, engagement is getting more difficult, especially as our newsfeeds become more cluttered. I usually ask people to follow my personal Facebook profile.

LinkedIn: I've found LinkedIn to be an awesome promotional tool, particularly if you are blogging or podcasting about a serious topic that has business appeal. Many of my connections will keep up with my updates and LinkedIn groups are a great way to interact with your target audience.

Google+: While in some ways, Google+ can seem like a ghost town, it's still an important network that can send your podcast traffic and increase your search engine rankings. I like Google+ communities, where you can discover others interested in your hobbies.

Pinterest: Primarily used by women, Pinterest is a unique platform that can drive massive referral traffic to a website that is image-centric and centered on the DIY/crafts niche. If your podcast is in this industry, I'd recommend checking out some relevant boards. Even though my other blog is not in this niche, I still use Pinterest to promote podcasts and posts on relevant boards.

Instagram: Unless you're part of a younger generation, it's likely you may be less familiar with Instagram than you are with Facebook. Instagram is a way to share your brand's story through images, quotes, and beautiful moments in your life.

SnapChat: Increasingly, I've seen snapchat being used by brands to promote messages, upcoming events, and develop rapport with their target audience. Although it may be a little premature, I think it's worth thinking about how you could integrate snapchat into a marketing strategy (people can follow you).

All these social networks might seem like a headache to manage! That's why I have used social media scheduling or automation tools like Hootsuite in the past. In fact, I have all my social media posts scheduled a month in advance! However, I keep my interactions, whether that's replying to tweets or retweeting, un-automated.

Banner Adverts

Banner advertisements are amongst the simplest form of advertising on the internet today. Basically, all you need to do is contact websites that are disseminating information about the topic that you have in mind for your podcast.

If you had a computer game podcast, you could approach websites and forums that computer gamers frequent. In fact, you can even directly approach the game's website itself and ask them to run your banners on their different pages and forums.

You can go for either a barter deal or a cash one with reference to your banners. In a barter deal, they can put up the banners of their websites on your site and allow you to do the same on theirs.

In case of a cash deal, you will have to pay them certain predetermined charges for displaying your banner on their site, just like an offline magazine. Your banner can contain the same tag line on every site so that the message will be reinforced every time users log on to sites where your banners are prominently displayed.

Here it's important to understand that the banner text must contain the tagline as well as the date and time of the first podcast. If you do not want to do that, simply clicking on the banner should transport them to your site so that they can get more information and sign up for updates if they're interested.

Get Your Own Website and Domain

It's 100% essential that you get your own website to accompany your podcast. I personally recommend:

Registering a domain first. You don't want to pick a podcast that doesn't have an available domain or that has a domain that is already in use by another company!

Getting a website host. I recommend setting up a Wordpress website. In order to do that, you're doing to need a hosting provider. I put together a free guide showing you how to set up a Wordpress website:

(http://www.salvadorbriggman.com/how-to-make-a-wordpress-website-step-by-step/)

WordPress will give you all the functionality to create a blog and website. There are a lot of free and premium templates out there.

You can also use an all-in-one solution like SquareSpace, Wix, or Webs. This might be an easy temporary solution, but long-term I think it pays huge dividends to know how to set up your own WordPress website. There are many plugins to extend the functionality of your website and you have complete control over the design.

Ultimately, you will be using your website to promote your podcast and maintain a relationship with your podcast listeners.

SEO (search engine optimization)

SEO is another easy way to market your podcast. As part of a strong SEO strategy, your website needs to include all the important keywords that you think your target audience may enter when they try and search for something online.

Basically, well-known search engines like Bing, Yahoo, Google etc. have algorithms working behind the scenes. These algorithms troll the world-wide web to deliver to the searcher the closest possible fits to the references he or she put into the search bar of the engine. If your website is SEO optimized, viola, your target audience ends up at your website.

Email and Newsletters

Despite the rise of social media, email is still the primary way that we receive and respond to information. My newsletter of 20,000+ people (my other blog) receives better click through rates and opens than any other marketing medium I use.

When random visitors come to your website who have discovered you on iTunes, social media, or through search engines, the only way that you will be able to form a long-lasting relationship with them is if you can contact them in some way.

Using an email list management tool like Aweber is a great way to begin building your email list in an organized way. These are people that you can notify about an upcoming podcast episode, or new products that you're coming out with!

I also use the analytics from email marketing campaigns to see which links people are interested in and what articles or podcasts they are clicking on. This helps inform the content choices I'll make in the future.

Blogging or Content Marketing

I think that blogging is the ultimate companion to podcasting! Some people love learning through reading. Others prefer audio. Having a blog gives them two choices!

In addition, it's no secret that blogging is the holy grail of gaining search engine traffic and building an audience. I recently detailed my experience building up my websites to over 1 million page views. I can tell you that if I didn't have some kind of blog or other way to communicate to the world in text form, this wouldn't have been possible.

Free content, whether that's in the form of a well-written blog article or ebook is also a great incentive for your readers to connect with you in other ways outside of your podcast. If the transcript of your podcast or the show notes for a particular episode are on your website, then it's likely they are going to take a second to check it out if they thought the episode was helpful.

Blog articles are also another form of content that you can schedule and promote on social media using Hootsuite, which will drive more people to your website (if the articles are helpful) and lead to more people checking out your podcast.

Lastly, if you have trouble coming up with blog article ideas, you can always re-purpose your audio content in the form of blog posts or re-purpose your blog posts in the form of a new podcast episode!

Go on Another Podcaster's Show

I have been a guest on the QNY Tech Podcast and others. Being a guest on other podcasts exposes your ventures to a larger audience and is another opportunity to improve your speaking abilities.

One of the great things about iTunes is that they also have a "Listeners also subscribed to" section. This means that cross-promotion between yourself and other podcasters can be beneficial to each of you.

Have Influencers on Your Podcast

Finally, having individuals on your podcast who are experts or have a large social network is another way to grow your podcast.

Each time you have a guest on your podcast, it will double the social reach of that episode (assuming they help promote it).

Leverage Show Mentions

What I mean by that is, if you mention someone during your show, send them an email and ask them to share the podcast episode!

If you have a guest on your show, specifically ask them to share the podcast when it comes out. You can't afford to be shy or just hope that they'll see it and share it. You need to be direct.

Drive Traffic to Previous Shows

Some of the podcast episodes that I did early in the year continue to get traffic. That's because I still promote and mention them.

According to Derek Halpern, an online marketer and entrepreneur, you should "Create content 20% of the time. Spend the other 80% of the time promoting what you created."

I agree with this statement, particularly for evergreen content or content that continues to hold its value over time.

It depends on the type of show that you have, but for me, if a I mention a topic I can say something along the lines of "and if you want to learn more about ____, check out episode ____."

Good Copywriting Improved My Download Numbers

The title of your episodes matter! The way in which you describe an episode matters. How you tease an episode matters!

When I deliberately took time to write good episode titles and write out attractive descriptions that highlighted the benefits of listening to a particular episode, my download number improved.

Remember, we live in a world that is competing for everyone's attention. Why should they listen to this episode? Why now? What value will it bring them?

This also holds true for the intro to a new episode, or when you mention another episode that the listener should check out. Always highlight what they'll get out of the experience.

Rank Well in a Marketplace, but Get People on Your Email List

There are huge benefits to ranking well in a marketplace like iTunes, Amazon, Google, or YouTube.

In a marketplace, there are visitors out to consume content and creators who produce it. When you rank well you'll be easier to find, and you'll have more authority for standing out among so many creators.

At the same time, you can't depend on your rankings in any marketplace that you don't control. Yes, this includes social media marketplaces like Twitter and Facebook.

Therefore, the only reliable way to build a sustainable audience is to get them on your email list. This way, you can continue to have a relationship with your audience, even if your rankings fall or your site crashes.

Having an email list has let me notify interested audience members of new episodes and drive traffic to specific episodes. It's a very powerful tool.

Consistency Creates Habit

Habit formation is the cornerstone of audience and customer development. Just think of McDonalds or Starbucks. People know what to expect, and are therefore much more likely to go to one of these locations then one they haven't heard of before.

In addition, people used to tune in at specific times on specific days to watch the news or TV shows because, over time, they learned that that's when they aired.

By putting out content consistently, you'll begin to develop habits in your audience. They'll know that if it's a Monday, there's bound to be a new show up, or that if it's Sunday and they're bored, you'll have a new show up soon.

Try not to leave your content creation to chance. I did this when I first started blogging.

Instead, create a schedule (ugh, I know it's not fun) and stick to it. It's effective if you want to be a serious creator or podcaster.

Provide Social Proof Around Specific Episodes

Remember, your goal isn't to market the podcast as a whole. Your goal should be to market specific episodes.

It's great to say that the podcast has been downloaded so many times or that you might have had such and such guests on, but why does this episode matter?

I found that a good way to provide social proof for my podcast is simply to communicate the credentials of the guest. Just because I know that this is a good guest doesn't mean that other people do.

Your tone of voice and speaking style will also add social proof to episodes. If you don't believe me, just think about how you'd speak differently if you had a major industry-related person on your podcast.

You'd be far more excited, which would make listeners more excited, and they'd realize that it's super lucky you got this guest to come on and it's going to be a great show.

The Art of the Ask: Get iTunes Reviews

I've read up on iTunes reviews. Some podcasters say that they play a big role in the algorithm. Others say that they don't play that big of a role.

Personally, I think that the frequency and newness of iTunes reviews do play a role in the iTunes marketplace algorithm.

So, how do you get more reviews? Ask specific people. Email them. Email your guests. Ask your friends. Ask your audience in the most direct way possible.

I've been experimenting with reading out reviews that I've gotten as a way to remind people to leave one themselves, or to add social proof to the show for new listeners.

I also highlight the benefits of leaving a review, like you might get a shout out, I use it as feedback, and it will help out the show, which is free.

Just by asking people and reminding listeners, I've been able to get 100+ reviews.

One of the Biggest Podcasting Mistakes to Avoid: Dismissing Marketing and Promotion

No one is going to toot your own horn for you. You need to get out there and form relationships with influencers or shout news from the roof tops.

There is this bias towards a "build it and they will come" mentality among content creators, myself included, which is just wrong. Yes, we put so much time, energy, and effort into creating great podcast content, but just because we know it's awesome doesn't mean that other people do!

I think that as more and more podcasters get into the niche, many will be disappointed when they don't see immediate results or when they find that they are trending one week in iTunes and forgotten about in the algorithm the next week.

You must be willing to promote your own podcast content, whether that's on other people's podcasts, through social media, or on your website.

Chapter 5: Monetizing Your Podcast

There are a few different ways that you can monetize your podcast. Some of these are more invasive than others, and depending on your niche or the topic/format of your podcast, one might be more effective than others. In this chapter, I'm going to go through some of the ways to make money from your podcast.

Sponsorships/Voice Ads

I have three sponsors on my podcast that are relevant to the audience. You might have heard other big-name podcasts sponsored by companies like Audible.com and 99Designs. Sponsorships are one way to monetize your podcast, though if you're going after one of the biggies, you need to have large download numbers.

Advertisements are priced on a CPM or cost per mile basis. One mile is 1,000 podcast downloads. This means that the number of downloads your show has will directly affect how much sponsorship income you rake in.

Sponsors will ask for the number of downloads per episode that your podcast receives in a six-week time frame. This is your expected download count if they purchase a sponsorship spot on your show.

For a fifteen second pre-roll advertisement, you can expect to make about $18 per 1,000 downloads. For a sixty second mid-roll advertisement, you can expect to make about $25 per 1,000 downloads.

Let's just say that your podcast averages 1,000 downloads per episode and you include two advertisers. Each of these advertisers have both a pre-roll and a mid-roll spot.

This means that you'll earn $86 per episode in sponsorship income. If you produced one show per week, you'd earn $4,472 per year in income from your show.

If your podcast averaged 25,000 downloads per episode and you included two advertisers as we stated above, you'd earn $2,150 per episode and $111,800 per year.

Podcasts are attractive to advertisers because the audience is hyper relevant and very attentive. After all, they're listening to a 30 to 60-minute-long show.

On the flip side, sponsorships are great for you because you'll command a high CPM compared to banner ads or other forms of advertising.

Affiliate Marketing

Affiliate marketing is simple. When you refer a customer to a business, they will give you a commission! Depending on the type of affiliate relationship, you could get a commission when someone signs up, clicks the link, or pays for the service.

The great thing about affiliate marketing is that you don't need to handle any of the customer service for the transaction. The company created the product and they service it. All you're doing it selling it.

There are a lot of online marketing blogs/podcasts like the SmartPassiveIncome website that are killing it with affiliate marketing. Using the pretty link plugin to customize a short link or Bitly links, podcast owners can easily track and refer visitors to an affiliate partner and receive commissions if anyone decides to buy on their site.

It might depend on the terms of service of the particular affiliate network whether or not they allow traffic to be re-directed or whether you must use one of the network's links and remember to plug the URL during your podcast. Either way, you could also direct visitors to a particular page on your podcast's website that contains affiliate links.

This may not be the best approach for a discussion-based podcast about politics or comedy, but it could be a great technique if you are teaching a subject to your listeners and they are eager to try out a product or service you've mentioned.

Inbound Marketing

Inbound marketing is when you use the podcast specifically as a lead generation tool. Having the podcast spreads awareness about you, your brand, and what you do. It could even simply serve as an introductory tool to high-net-worth guests that you bring on the show.

Either way, you're using the podcast as a way to get your foot in the door. You're not trying to make money directly from the show, but rather from the relationships the show opens up.

One time, I was on a podcast and the host told me that he only does the show because it leads to lucrative speaking gigs. The people who hire him as a speaker are always impressed that he runs a show that interviews entrepreneurs. He doesn't make much money from the actual show, but he makes five figures from his speaking career.

A good example of inbound marketing is the Rainmaker FM podcast network, which is providing a tremendous amount of value to its listeners. In exchange for providing value, they have the opportunity to push or make the public more aware about their own product or service, which could be beneficial.

The key to this monetization approach is to deliver relevant value, build a relationship over time, and get readers onto your webpage or to interact outside of the passive listening medium. It's also important to deliver high quality information, otherwise rather than looking like an expert in your field, you'll look like an amateur.

If you're unfamiliar with inbound marketing both through podcasting and blogging/social media, I'd check out Gary Vaynerchuk's book, Jab, Jab, Jab, Right Hook: How to Tell Your Story in a Noisy Social World. I also learned a lot from Seth Godin's book, Permission Marketing: Turning Strangers into Friends and Friends into Customers.

Paid Podcast App or Premium Content

You could create a paid app that users must download if they'd like to listen to your podcast. This could be to accompany some kind of online course, part of a membership website, or standalone app in of itself.

When listeners sign up for this, they're getting convenience or value that they couldn't get elsewhere. Your solution is saving them time, money, and headache.

Keep in mind that you will be competing with many free podcasts in the iTunes store, so figuring out why your listeners care about you and your material is vital. Paid content is becoming commonplace in the online world and it's only a matter of time before this begins to permeate the audio world as well.

Products and Services

One of the ways that I monetize my podcast is with my own products and services, including books, online courses, coaching, and more.

Since listeners are already warmed up to you and the value you bring to their life, they're more willing to check out your products than if you just met them on the street.

You can even create your own digital or physical products that you can sell to the listeners of the podcast. This could also include t-shirts that you create with a website like TeeSpring.

Crowdfunding

Finally, you can also use a crowdfunding platform like Patreon or JoyRide as a way for your audience to help support the show and be rewarded for it. This could be an interesting way to both engage your listeners and thank them for being a valued member of your podcast's community.

Patreon works as both a donation website and a premium content locker. Basically, you can offer exclusive content to your audience when they donate to help with the production of the show. Depending on how much the pledge to your Patreon campaign, they'll unlock different benefits or exclusive offerings.

You can use Patreon and other crowdfunding websites to help fund the production of your show and bring your community closer together.

How to Approach Monetization

For beginners, podcasting is the same as every other industry out there. Often times, beginners can become overzealous about the income potential of running a successful show and be blinded about what it takes to get there.

The most important thing is to produce quality episodes on a regular basis until you gain a small following. Once you're seeing regular downloads of your show, you can begin to think more seriously about monetization.

I would first concentrate on getting your show to 100 downloads per episode. Then, work to grow it to 500 downloads per episode. At that point, you'll be able to begin to make money with the show using some of the techniques I discussed above.

Big sponsors will only begin to look at shows once you've proven that they can get thousands and thousands of downloads per episode. They're not interested in sponsoring a show that only gets 1,000 or 2,000 downloads.

During your first 25 to even 50 episodes, you'll mainly be learning. You'll be figuring out how to promote the episodes, write effective titles, speak with confidence, obtain high quality guests, and ask your guests intriguing questions.

It takes an entire system to produce a great show. You need an intro, conclusion, and some sound editing. If you're cross posting the show on a blog or website, you also need to write effective copy to get people to listen to the show. Then, you gotta get out there and promote it.

Your initial efforts should be spent streamlining this system. You'll begin to discover how you can produce shows more easily and faster. This initial learning is vital to the overall growth of your podcast. As you begin to scale, you'll use this system to make sure your episodes continue to come out on a regular basis.

Once you've finally mastered the basics of podcasting and you are beginning to gather a bit of an audience, then you need to switch your mindset. You need to then begin to treat your podcast like a business.

If you want to earn a full-time income from podcasting, then you need to work at it with the same level of dedication and commitment that you would a full-time job. Yes, I mean you should work 40 hours per week (minimum) at growing the show.

The recipe for earning small amounts of money from a podcast is to treat it just like a hobby. When you have a hobby, you work at it sometimes and only when you really feel like it. It's fun, but you're not totally committed.

To seriously turn this into your full-time job, you're going to need to take it seriously. Set aside a budget and invest in the business. Work hard each day and produce quality work. Don't make excuses. This is a surefire way for seeing massive progress in a short amount of time.

For much of my 20s, I treated my blog, my podcast, and my YouTube channel as a fun lifestyle business. I didn't take it seriously. I woke up when I felt like it (sometimes at 11 am or 12 pm). I partied late into the night with my friends.

While I was able to see a certain level of success based on my talent alone, I realized I was hindering my own progress. I came to the conclusion that I wanted more in life. I decided to spend more of my free time growing my business and working to improve myself.

This is the burden of free time. When you get it up and running, podcasting will unlock tons of free time. You can spend it traveling, playing with your kids, or reading books. You'll finally be your own boss and live a life of freedom. Just remember that if you want to see growth over the years, you have to continue to invest back into the process.

Chapter 6: Conclusion

The opportunity is there. Podcasts are replacing radio as the go-to listening medium for commuters. For the price of a low-cost microphone, you can get in front of an audience of thousands of people and share your message with the world.

I know that it's scary. I was afraid to put myself out there too. I didn't know what people would think or how they would react.

My first few episodes were horrible. I sounded terribly meek and my questions to show guests weren't that great. But, I kept at it. I kept publishing new shows.

I'm so glad I did. It transformed my entire online business. The podcast is directly responsible for bringing new customers and clients in the door. It has even led to exclusive speaking gigs.

From the bottom of my heart, I want you to launch a successful show (and reach out to me as a podcasting success story).

I sincerely hope that reading this book is a small part in that journey. I hope you've found this book to be helpful. If you have, can you please take a second to rate and review it on Amazon. A good review would mean the world to me.

Also, if you'd like to gain access to a video I have revealing more podcasting tips for beginners and I'll link you to it here: http://www.salvadorbriggman.com/podcastinghacksbonus

Happy Podcasting!

Salvador Briggman

"I learned many great lessons from my father, not the least of which was that you can fail at what you don't want, so you might as well take a chance on doing what you love." - Jim Carrey

About the Author

Salvador Briggman founded the popular blog, CrowdCrux, which has been cited by the New York Times, The Wallstreet Journal, CNN, and more. He helps entrepreneurs raise money on crowdfunding platforms like Kickstarter and Indiegogo. Last year, he helped nearly 400,000 individuals raise money from the crowd through his website, products, newsletter, and forum.

Salvador also runs a popular podcast, Crowdfunding Demystified, which has been downloaded more than 150,000 times. He has interviewed millionaire entrepreneurs, authors, influencers, and the award-winning podcaster, John Lee Dumas.

Made in the USA
San Bernardino, CA
15 March 2019